MW01196672

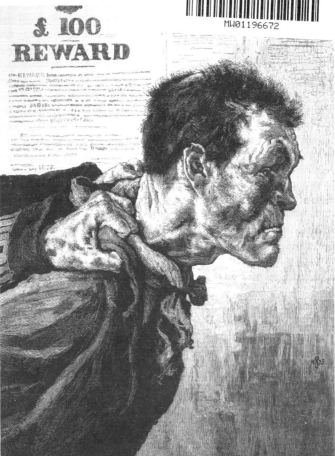

This US edition © Wooden Books Ltd 2025
Published by Wooden Books LLC,
San Rafael, California

First published in the UK in 2022
by Wooden Books Ltd, Glastonbury, UK

Library of Congress Cataloging-in-Publication Data
Jones, A.
Character

Library of Congress Cataloging-in-Publication
Data has been applied for

ISBN-10: 1-952178-40-1
ISBN-13: 978-1-952178-40-5

All rights reserved
For permission to reproduce any part of this
character-building book please contact the publishers

Designed and typeset in Glastonbury, UK

Printed in India on FSC® certified papers by
Quarterfold Printabilities Pvt. Ltd.

CHARACTER
ARCS AND ARCHETYPES

Amy Jones

Dedicated to
Bryony Quinn and Tiffany Chadha
in celebration of positive arcs in 2023

Thanks to my exceptional editor Stephen Parsons.
Recommended further reading: *Character*: *Three Inquiries in Literary Studies*, Amanda Anderson, Rita Felski, and Toril Moi; *The Art of Fiction: A Guide for Writers and Readers*, Ayn Rand; *Hero with a Thousand Faces,* Joseph Campbell*; The Writer's Journey,* Christopher Vogler; *Aspects of the Novel*, EM Forster; *The Danger of a Single Story*, Chimamanda Adichie; *The Writer's Guide to Character Traits*, Linda N. Edelstein; *The Craft of Writing*; William Sloane.

Introduction   1

History of Character   2

Types of Character: Flat Characters   4

  Round Characters   6

  Dynamic vs Static   8

  Archetypes   10

  Protagonists & Antagonists   12

  Heroes & Heroines   14

  Antiheroes   16

  Villains   18

  Confidants & Foils   20

Psychology: What Kind of Person?   22

  Motivation & Agency   24

  Frustration & Conflict   26

  Flaws, Wounds & Secrets   28

Development: Character Arcs   30

  Positive Growth Arcs   32

  Declining Arcs   34

Characterisation: Inventing Character   36

  Appearance   38

  Environment   40

  Action & Reaction   42

  Thoughts   44

Speech: Dialogue   46

  Dialect   48

  Real Speech   50

  Natural or Real?   52

Planning: Sketches & Summary   54

  Character Profiles   56

Theophrastus's Characters

1. The DISSEMBLER – a liar/untrustworthy
2. The ADULATOR/flatterer – makes you cringe.
3. The GARRULOUS – talks at great length on matters irrelevant, trivial, or inappropriate.
4. The RUSTIC/boor – indecorous, he wears his shoes too large for his feet and talks in a loud voice.
5. The PLAUSIBLE – 'He will attend you a little way, and ask when he is to see you, and will take his leave with a compliment upon his lips.'
6. The RUFFIAN/reckless – 'troublesome persons' who create unrest wherever they go, quick to engage in or permit immoral behaviour.
7. The LOQUACIOUS – a chatterbox.
8. The FABRICATOR of News – a gossip.
9. The SORDID – spits while talking, nose blowing at the table, nail biting during sacrifice.
10. The SHAMELESS – one who is willing to sell their reputation or morals for base gain.
11. The PENURIOUS – tight fisted when it comes to finance, obsessed with petty gains.
12. The IMPURE – one of poor manners, loud, brash and inconsiderate.
13. The UNSEASONABLE – well intentioned, but mistimed in actions, engaging the busy in conversation, complaining about relationships at a wedding.
14. The OFFICIOUS – hinders and annoys with his affected good intentions, little actual benefit.
15. The STUPID – lacking in wit, liable to misread situations or express themselves poorly/inaccurately
16. The SURLY – quick tempered. "Don't bother me"
17. The SUPERSTITIOUS – fears misfortune, avoids cracks in pavements, black cats, ladders.
18. The PETULANT – a petty complainer who always perceives themselves as hard done by.
19. The SUSPICIOUS/distrustful – considers everyone as a potential enemy or threat.
20. The FILTHY – an unclean person 'will use rancid oil to anoint himself at the bath; and go forth ... wearing a thick tunic, and light cloak, covered with stains'.
21. The DISAGREEABLE – a quietly annoying person, who over a long period would infuriate a person more perhaps that the more overly unpleasant characters.
22. The VAIN – one of petty ambition who feels they deserve better than their neighbour.
23. The PENURIOUS - Tight fisted and mean, he will pour the smallest libation to Artemis and forbid his wife to lend a neighbour salt or a lampwick.
24. The OSTENTATIOUS - The absurd vanity of the purse proud man leads him to make as many false pretensions to wealth as the veriest knave who lives by seeming to be what he is not.
25. The PROUD - The proud man regards the whole human race with contempt; himself excepted.
26. The FEARFUL - a dejection of the spirits, which renders them liable to the constant tyranny of fear.
27. The OLD TRIFLER - This foolish fellow, although he is threescore; would fain distinguish himself in accomplishments and exercises proper only to youth.
28. The DETRACTOR - utters not a word that does not betray the malignancy of his soul.
29. The OLIGARCH - An arrogant desire to dominate over his fellows appears in the opinions, the conduct, and the manners of this partisan of despotism.
30. The MALIGNANT - The good he defames and persecutes; the bad alone he applauds.

THEOPHRASTUS, a student of Aristotle in the late fourth century BC, wrote a collection of thirty sketches classifying different categories of character one might encounter on the streets of Athens.

INTRODUCTION

WHO IS YOUR FAVORITE character in literature or film? What is it about them which makes them memorable? From twinkly-eyed Mrs Tiggywinkle, to gruff Mr Darcy, savage Heathcliff and morally upstanding Atticus Finch, great characters last through the ages and persist as cultural reference points. Before you mould your own leading character from the clay of your words, consider too your antagonists, confidants, foils and other supporting members of the cast, all essential elements in good storytelling. How you position them all within your story will depend partly on whether you are developing a plot-led narrative or a character-led one, or maybe you aim to skillfully use both—an approach which perhaps defines the very best fiction. My companion books *Plot* and *Narrative* contain more information.

This little book explores the different types and functions of character found in film, literature and television, and explains some of the techniques authors use to create their palettes of characters. We will explore character development and arcs, idiosyncrasies of movement and speech and technical aspects of writing effective and convincing dialogue, as well as archetypal roles, pyscho-emotional complexities, backstories and profiles. You will learn how to breathe life into your creations, give them complex inner lives equipped for emotional journeys that we all recognize, and bring them to life on the page. So be prepared:

> The moment when a character does or says something you hadn't thought about. At that moment he's alive and you leave him to it. Graham Greene

History of Character
from types to individuation

The word 'character' comes from the Greek *charassein*, 'to engrave', and is not used in the sense of an 'imagined person in a creative work' until the 17th century. Accordingly, the characters we meet in Greek drama and European folk tales are mostly 'types', albeit with inner struggles and recognisable PERSONALITY TRAITS (*see Theophrastus, page vi*).

In his *Poetics*, Aristotle states that characters in a play must be an integral part of the plot, a functional element of the story:

> For a thing whose presence or absence makes no visible difference, is not an organic part of the whole. Aristotle, Poetics, 300BC

He says that characters should act with VERISIMILITUDE (they should seem to be real), CONSISTENCY (they should have reliable traits) and PROPRIETY (they should behave appropriately to their role). And they should be:

> noble or base, since human character regularly conforms to these distinctions, all of us being different in character because of some quality of goodness or evil.

One of the earliest character-led works in the European tradition, Apuleius' *Metamorphoses* (*The Golden Ass*), appears in Latin in the 2nd century AD. The 11th century Japanese work *The Tale of Genji* by Murasaki Shikibu has notable psychological REALISM. We move a step closer to INDIVIDUATED characters with Shakespeare [1564–1616]:

> ... the man who of all Modern, and perhaps Ancient Poets [who] needed not the spectacles of Books to read Nature; he look'd inwards, and found her there.
>
> John Dryden

His heroes, kings, queens, fools, and lovers are imbued with idiosyncratic conflicts and inconsistencies. King Lear, for example, has:

> This depth of nature, this force of passion, this tug and war of the elements of our being, this firm faith in filial piety, and the giddy anarchy and whirling tumult of the thoughts ... William Hazlitt, *Characters of Shakespear's Plays*, 1817

Hazlitt also muses on Hamlet's speeches and sayings, concluding:

> They are as real as our own thoughts... It is we who are Hamlet.

By the early 18th century, as concepts of individual freedom begin to exert influence in wider society, eponymous works like *Robinson Crusoe* [1719] and *Moll Flanders* [1722] depict more socially diverse **PROTAGONISTS** (*see page 12*) with unique perspectives. Later epistolary novels, such as Samuel Richard's *Pamela* [1740] and *Clarissa* [1749] induce:

> readers to empathize with ordinary people; it forces readers to see that the most ordinary people, even servants like Pamela, the heroine of Richardson's novel of that name, have inner selves just like their own. Lynn Hunt

By the time of Sterne's 1759 novel *Tristam Shandy*, character had became the soul of fiction; 'types' still had a role but were no longer foundational. The stage was set for modern character, in all its individual, emotional, and archetypal glory. At its heart, the concepts of **EMPATHY** and **MIMESIS**.

ABOVE: *Greek actors wore masks (a* **PERSONA***) to project specific personality traits.*

3

FLAT CHARACTERS
and stock stereotypes

While the portrayal of character has deepened over the centuries, there is always a place for cardboard cutouts. These mostly one- or two-dimensional beings are known as **FLAT CHARACTERS**. They may play some **FUNCTIONAL** role in a narrative, but generally lack any depth of personality. Thus we know little or nothing of how they came to be as they are (so have no **BACKSTORY**) and we see no change in them over the course of the story (they have no **CHARACTER DEVELOPMENT**). In the words of E.M. Forster, flat characters, like the pieces on a chessboard:

> *... never need reintroducing, never run away, have not to be watched for development, and provide their own atmosphere ...* Aspects of the Novel, 1927

A good novel often requires flat characters as well as more rounded ones (*see page 6*), and the outcome of their collisions can add realism to your writing. They can also be useful **FOILS** (*see page 20*).

Flat characters may have some all-encompassing motivation which serves a specific goal or supports another character:

> *The really flat character can be expressed in one sentence such as, "I will never desert Mr Micawber." There is Mrs Micawber - she says she won't desert Mr Micawber; she doesn't, and there she is.* E. M. Forster

This one dimensionality can, as in the example above, also make them powerful providers of comic, but never tragic, relief.

Flat characters are often off-the-shelf **STOCK CHARACTERS**, who exist merely for a specific narrative purpose, e.g.: *Innkeeper of the local tavern, a collector of gossip and Toby jugs.* Generally a **TROPE** of their genre, they can be useful narrative devices. Used in Ancient Greece, notably by Theophrastus (*see page vi*) and his student Menander, stock characters have been built up over time, as narratives are told and retold.

In Italian COMMEDIA DELL'ARTE, actors played a familiar cast of stock characters, such as the INNAMORATI (two young and passionate lovers), IL DOTTORE (a pontificating professional man), PULCINELLA (the melancholic misanthropic), COLUMBINA (the quick-witted servant) and PANTALONE (the miserly wealthy merchant), in various improvised scenarios. Each character had its recognisable costume, mannerisms, and voice; many also had masks (*see below*). Their influence on the comedies of Shakespeare is evident in characters like the bumbling officer Dogberry in *Much Ado About Nothing*.

Pantomime is also replete with stock characters; a FAIRY GODMOTHER *aiding* the hero(ine), a WICKED STEPMOTHER *obstructing*. In modern fiction, characters like the authoritarian principal in the film *Ferris Bueller's Day Off* have oppositional functions, while a kindly, bespectacled librarian like Mrs Phelps in Roald Dahl's *Matilda* will offer assistance.

Other examples of stock clichéd characters, or ARCHETROPES, include: *The Loner; Hardboiled Detective; Bad Boy; Damsel in Distress; Boy or Girl Next Door; Tough Cop; Innocent Child; Evil Genius; Party Head; Plain Jane; Blind Seer; Sleazy Politician; Hopeless Romantic; Geeky Nerd; Starving Artist; Femme Fatale; Outlaw;* and *Mad Scientist.*

ROUND CHARACTERS
complex and surprising

ROUND CHARACTERS, the main subject of this book, are three-dimensional complex individuals with strong personal traits and clear driving forces. They engage readers and audiences, invoking strong emotional responses through their actions, developments and eventual fates:

> *The test of a round character is whether it is capable of surprising in a convincing way. If it never surprises, it is flat. If it does not convince, it is a flat pretending to be round.* E. M. Forster, *Aspects of the Novel*, 1927

The surprise does not have to be earth-shattering. A character who is only ever a receptionist sitting behind a desk in an office is flat. But if she *Surprise!* also dreams of being an artist, and *Surprise!* doesn't love her fiancée, but *Surprise!* is in love with another person in the office, and *Surprise!* has a wicked sense of humour too, she becomes a round character and a major role in the 2001 BBC TV comedy *The Office*.

To ensure your round characters really are round, try asking these six questions of them (here with Jay Gatsby as an example):

1. **WHAT INTERNAL CONFLICT ARE THEY STRUGGLING WITH?** Gatsby struggles internally with his love for Daisy and his sense of class inferiority – despite his wealth he can never truly be a part of her 'set'.

2. **WHAT EXTERNAL FORCES ARE THEY IN CONFLICT WITH?** Gatsby is in external conflict with Tom Buchanan, Daisy's husband

3. **WHAT MOTIVATES THEM? WHAT DO THEY DESIRE?** Gatsby is motivated by the American Dream. He wants to accrue wealth and status, to obtain Daisy – because of love and/or what she represents to him.

4. **WHAT IS THEIR BACKSTORY?** Real name James Gatz, born to poor parents. Dropped out of school. Protegee to a copper tycoon but is cheated out of inheritance. Joins the army during WW1 and meets Daisy during training. Serves and becomes a major in the war. May have briefly attended Oxford University (or not). Returns to America and makes his fortune as a bootlegger during the prohibition.

5. **WHAT RECOGNISABLE TRAITS DO THEY EMBODY?** Social insecurity, desire to be liked and admired by others, and wanting to be loved by a beautiful young woman.

6. **HOW DO THEY SURPRISE US?** With his past, his generosity and flamboyance, his questionable friends, his untruths, his noble—if misguided—sacrifice at the end of the novel, and the realisation that despite his many flaws he might be 'better' than all the other characters.

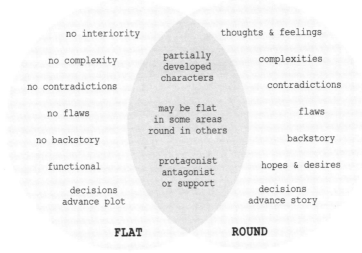

FLAT / ROUND diagram

FLAT
- no interiority
- no complexity
- no contradictions
- no flaws
- no backstory
- functional
- decisions advance plot

(overlap)
- partially developed characters
- may be flat in some areas round in others
- protagonist antagonist or support

ROUND
- thoughts & feelings
- complexities
- contradictions
- flaws
- backstory
- hopes & desires
- decisions advance story

DYNAMIC VS STATIC
do they undergo change?

"Change is good" goes the saying, but not everyone does change. The personality and internal growth of **STATIC CHARACTERS** remain unchanged over the course of a story. However, this does not necessarily mean they are uninteresting. **STATIC FLAT** characters are often the central figures in serialized works. Hercule Poirot, for example, is always the same

> *short, pernickety, somewhat vain, Belgian detective with a waxed moustache, relying on his "little grey cells" to solve crimes ...*

Agatha Christie resets her detectives at the end of each work so that she can pick up again without having to worry about continuity in later adventures—you can read her whodunnits in any order.

Sherlock Holmes, meanwhile, is a more rounded character, and yet he too does not change. He remains clever, analytical, and emotionally detached throughout the various stories. Albus Dumbledore is another **STATIC ROUND** character. We know his backstory, his complexities, his desires, and his flaws, but he does not undergo significant change.

DYNAMIC CHARACTERS develop during a narrative, undergoing change, either positive or negative, in personality or outlook. They have **CHARACTER ARCS** (*see pages 30–34*). Scout Finch, the protagonist in Harper Lee's 1960 novel *To Kill a Mockingbird*, is profoundly altered after she gains an understanding of the racial injustice endemic in her community.

Most dynamic characters are also round characters. Fanny Burney's 1778 novel *Evelina* follows her **DYNAMIC ROUND** heroine on a trajectory of positive development, overcoming various challenges or threats along the way to 'come of age' in Georgian society, and happily marry.

Most flat characters are static. However, both Ebenezer Scrooge in Dickens' *A Christmas Carol*, and the beast in *Beauty and the Beast* change profoundly, despite us knowing little about them. Instead, their change is *the* essential component of the plot, so they can be thought of as evolving from flat characters to more rounded ones.

Characters often grow in one area and remain unchanged in another, displaying both dynamic and static traits (*see below*)—a balance of consistency and realism that satisfies Aristotle's maxims (*see page 2*).

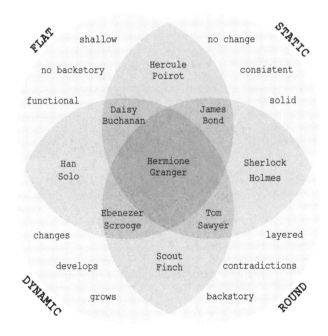

ARCHETYPES
the universal faces

We all recognize a hero, right from when we are small, and we all know a rotten egg when we see one. Some types of characters appear over and over again, in life and in art. An **ARCHETYPE** is a class of universal pattern originally developed by Swiss psychologist Carl Jung [1875–1961]:

> *The primordial image, or archetype, is a figure—be it a daemon, a human being, or a process—that constantly recurs in the course of history and appears wherever creative fantasy is freely expressed. Essentially, therefore, it is a mythological figure.* The Archetypes and the Collective Unconscious, 1951.

For screenwriter Christopher Vogler archetypes are flexible character functions which can be used to liberate your storytelling. They are:

> *... part of the universal language of storytelling, and a command of their energy is as essential to the writer as breathing.* The Writer's Journey, 1992.

While individual characters may embody specific archetypes—such as a **HERO** protagonist (**HIGHER SELF**), a **VILLAIN** antagonist (**SHADOW**), or a **CONFIDENT** deuteragonist (**ALLY**)—the archetypes can also appear as

> *masks, worn by the characters temporarily as they are needed to advance the story. ... Ideally, every well-rounded character should manifest a touch of every archetype, because the archetypes are expressions of the parts that make up a complete personality.* Christopher Vogler. The Writer's Journey, 1992.

Thus the **HERO** or **HEROINE** (the main character, or *protagonist, p.12*):

> *... learns from the other characters, fusing them into a complete human being.*

To achieve this, she or he will need the following:

1. RELATABLE QUALITIES (e.g. courage / strength / kindness).
2. UNIVERSAL DRIVES (e.g. desire to be loved / understood / avenged).
3. COMPLEX EMOTIONAL RESPONSES (and at times conflicting ones).
4. FLAWED ASPECTS of personality (e.g. quirks / weaknesses / vices).
5. AGENCY (the ability to perform the decisive action in the story).

We will explore these themes further in the pages which follow.

Mentor
Teacher, protector. *Brings knowledge, wisdom, selflessness.* (Athena, Virgil, Merlin, Gandalf, Yoda; also the Dark Mentor)

Higher Self
Deepest aspect of self. *Authenticity, purpose.* (Socrates, Beatrice, Galadriel, Siddhartha)

Shapeshifter
Friend or foe? *Teaches adaptability, ambiguity, deception.* (Zeus, Circe, Gollum, The White Witch, Carmen Sternwood)

Ally
Traveling companion, friend, foil. *Loyalty, kindness, empathy.* (Patroclus, Horatio, Dr Watson, Samwise Gamgee, Chewbacca, Ron & Hermione)

HERO

Threshold Guardian
Gatekeeper, protector. *Teaches the overcoming of obstacles & fears, trust, confidence.* (Cerberus, Charon, the Sphinx, Morpheus, Hagrid)

Trickster
Disrupter, challenger. *Teaches wit, charm, humour, unorthodoxy, magic.* (Puck, Loki, The Joker, Jack Sparrow, Reynard the Fox, Bart Simpson)

Shadow
The Antagonist, dark side. Anguish. *Teaches courage and integration.* (Macbeth, Iago, Caliban, Kurtz, Dracula, Mr Hyde, Sauron, Voldemort)

Herald. Call to adventure. *Responsibility*

Love Interest. *Ethics, emotional growth.*

Outcast. Prejudice, *Contrast, generosity.*

ABOVE: The primary archetypes, as developed by Joseph Campbell and Christopher Vogler.

Protagonists & Antagonists
and deuteragonists and tritagonists

The **PROTAGONIST** (Greek 'lead actor') is the character in a work of fiction who typically faces the main conflict or obstacle in the story and as a result undergoes a significant transformation. There are three types:

1. **THE HERO** *is someone we root for and can relate to. A central character with obvious virtues, strengths, flaws, and weaknesses (see pages 10-11 and 14-15).*

2. **THE ANTI-HERO** *lacks many traditional heroic qualities, and may even have some villainous traits, but can act heroically if required (see pages 16-17). If brought down by their own flaws they become a **TRAGIC HERO**.*

3. **THE VILLAIN** *can be the lead character, although more often they appear as an antagonist in opposition to a hero protagonist (see pages 18-19).*

The protagonist drives the narrative forward through their actions and decisions. They often have goals, and their journey towards achieving these forms the backbone of the story. Their fate matters the most to us.

To avoid rabbit holes, identify who your core protagonist is before you begin writing. You may have two central characters (e.g. *Antony & Cleopatra*, *Thelma & Louise*), or a multi-protagonist narrative like Chimamanda Adichie's *Half of a Yellow Sun*, allowing you to explore the same events from multiple perspectives. These can be challenging to construct but, as Adichie explains, the danger of a single story is that it:

> *creates stereotypes, and the problem with stereotypes is not that they are untrue, but that they are incomplete. They make one story become the only story.*

You may also opt for an **ENSEMBLE CAST**, such as those found in multi-season TV series where different episodes focus on different characters.

DEUTERAGONISTS are *secondary characters* (or 'secondary mains') who have significant interactions with the protagonist, providing insight into their motivations and personality. They may also have their own relationships or conflicts with other characters in the story, adding depth and complexity to the narrative. They may be a VICTIM. Many of the archetypes we met on the previous page are expressed within these characters, supporting or antagonizing a protagonist's journey.

The TRITAGONIST was once the third most important person in Greek drama. They are now more commonly referred to as minor or *tertiary characters*, used as foils (*p.20*), companions, catalysts, stock symbols, or to provide atmosphere.

The ANTAGONIST (Greek 'anti-actor') is the character who stands in opposition to the protagonist, and creates conflict in the story. Narratives feed on CONFLICT, and antagonists provide it—they antagonize.

Antagonistic forces can take the form of villains (*see pages 18–19*), love interests, family members, authority figures, societal forces, external forces (like nature or capitalism), and inner conflicts (like conscience):

> *Oh God! what could I do? I foamed — I raved — I swore! ... "Villains!"*
> *I shrieked, "dissemble no more! I admit the deed!* Edgar Allan Poe, The Tell Tale Heart

The sea in *Robinson Crusoe* is a classic non-human antagonist:

> *... the wind began to blow and the sea to rise in a most frightful manner;*
> *I was most inexpressibly sick in body and terrified in mind...* Daniel Defoe, 1719

Many conflict creators lack malice; they just have goals opposed to the protagonist's. In *Pride and Prejudice*, authority figures Mrs. Bennet and Lady de Bourgh try to prevent Elizabeth from marrying the man she loves.

HEROES & HEROINES
leading from the front, ready or not

Some people shine. The original hero (Greek 'protector') was the demigod Gilgamesh, king of Uruk around 2700BC. The Greek heroes Hercules and Achilles were also demigods, as were the early Indian heroes Lord Rama and Lord Krishna. Today, figures like this are known as EPIC HEROES.

> *As when from the high crest of a great mountain a glittering spring runs clear off, running in the wind's path down a dark gorge, so Achilles glittered in the bronze like a stream of water running down from a thunderstorm, shining far off in the sunlight, and he came on fast, leaving his huts behind him, and at heart was eager to cross into the forefront of battle where Trojans and Achaeans were fighting each other, giving one another strength-destroying blows.* Homer, Iliad, c.750BC

While heroes and heroines can come in all shapes and sizes (*see opposite*), they are often admired for possessing at least some heroic qualities, like courage, resilience, selflessness, achievements, resilience, wisdom, or moral purpose. Many heroes are flawed, and are hard to categorize. For example, the brooding BYRONIC HERO can be considered an offshoot of the ROMANTIC HERO, the TRAGIC HERO, or even a form of ANTI HERO (*see pages 16–17*), as here with Emily Brontë's tortured hero Heathcliff:

> *I have a single wish, and my whole being and faculties are yearning to attain it. They have yearned towards it so long, and so unwaveringly, that I'm convinced it will be reached — and soon — because it has devoured my existence: I am swallowed up in the anticipation of its fulfilment.* Emily Brontë, Wuthering Heights, 1847

Heroes can be WILLING (King Arthur) or RELUCTANT (Bilbo Baggins), EPIC (Odysseus) or EVERYMAN (Jane Eyre), GROUP-ORIENTED (Jason and the Argonauts) or a LONER (Sherlock Holmes). Some heroes are primarily CATALYSTS, but almost all of them experience GROWTH, SACRIFICE, and some form of CONFRONTATION WITH DEATH (or similar, such as a loss in a high-stakes game, or the end of a relationship).

EPIC HERO
· *Incredibly brave / wise*
· *Has one weakness*
· *Great physical strength*
· *Descended / blessed by gods*
(Hercules, Sita, Antigone,
Achilles, Beowulf, Superman)

ROMANTIC HERO
· *Emotionally sensitive*
· *Idealist in a cruel world*
· *Rebels against social norms*
· *Seeks to find meaning*
(Elizabeth Bennet, Sir Lancelot,
Jane Eyre, Cyrano de Bergerac)

BYRONIC HERO
· *Dark, brooding, passionate*
· *Sophisticated, attractive*
· *Haunted by a dark past*
· *Morally dubious*
(Anna Karenina, Mr Rochester,
Madame Bovary, Severus Snape)

EVERYMAN HERO
· *Ordinary life / job / looks*
· *Empathic / down to earth*
· *Struggles in role as 'hero'*
· *Usually triumphs in some way*
(Winston Smith, Tess Durbeyfield,
Leopold Bloom, Arthur Dent)

TRAGIC HERO (trad)
· *Noble or divine birth*
· *Virtuous, Courageous*
· *Flawed, or makes error(s)*
· *Avoidable death*
(Electra, Oedipus, Cleopatra,
Hamlet, Romeo, Juliet, King Lear)

TRAGIC HERO (modern)
· *Varied social background*
· *Flawed, e.g. obsessive*
· *Brave but can lack agency*
· *May/not have downfall*
(Scarlett O'Hara, Willy Loman,
Raskolnikov, Sherlock Holmes)

NAIVE HERO
· *Inexperienced, vulnerable*
· *Strong moral compass*
· *Open-hearted, selfless*
· *Propelled by external forces*
(Prince Myshkin, Forest Gump, Don
Quixote, Dorothea Brooke)

PROMETHEAN HERO
· *Idealistic, hubristic*
· *Visionary but lacks judgement*
· *Oversteps human boundaries*
· *Ends badly*
(Dante, Dr Jekyll, Victor
Frankenstein, Dr. Moreau)

ABOVE: Hero protagonists, ancient and modern. Categorisation is not always simple.

ANTIHEROES

the good, the bad, and the ugly

We all experience conflict between right and wrong. **ANTIHEROES** are complex characters who embody the struggle between the light and shadow sides of nature, and occupy the grey area between hero and villain. In late 18th and 19th century works, antiheroes were mostly villains or antagonists with narrative focalisation; in contemporary works, driven by postmodern perspectives, antiheroes have become more nuanced and sophisticated, and now often take the role of protagonist, centre stage.

Antiheroes often have a compelling backstory, and struggle to overcome or reconcile morally dubious qualities. They embody the archetypal elements of **SHADOW** and **TRICKSTER**, subverting norms and bringing

```
                        HERO - ANTIHERO
                    Idealist - Realist
      Conformist, peacekeeper - Dissident, agitator
         Stands up to baddies - Stands up to authority
 Bravely faces conflict head-on - Tries to get around conflict
   Motivated by pure intentions - Driven by basic urges
Classically handsome or beautiful - Rough or unusual-looking
        Always gets the girl/boy - Not interested in love's rewards
    Possesses gifts and talents - Nothing special about them
       Conventional moral values - Idiosyncratic moral compass
        On the right side of the law - Has little respect for the law
Always proactive, makes decisions - Often passive, pushed into things
      Very much looks the hero - Swears, drinks, sleeps around
 Succeeds at goals, unless tragic - Often fails, unless redeemed
         Seeks to overcome flaws - Fond of their flaws
              The Hero Changes - The Antihero is unchanged
        Serves the greater good - Driven by self-interest
        Knight on White Steed - Fallen Angel
```

ABOVE: *Contrasts between Hero and Antihero (after Ehlers, VanFoseen & Bond).*

subterranean aspects of personality to the surface. This can produce positive results if they are more hero than villain, or negative consequences if they slide towards the dark side.

A subcategory of antiheroes illustrate just how high these stakes are. FAUSTIAN BARGAINERS make deals with devils in exchange for immediate material, physical or intellectual gain. However, forever beholden, they pay a heavy price and rue the day they made the agreement. Marlowe's Faustus finds himself dragged to hell by demons, Goethe's Faust makes it to heaven, but only at considerable personal cost.

Like heros, antiheroes often slip and slide between categories (*below*). We don't always like them, but we are mostly sympathetic to their inner contradictions and turmoil. They are very human, and that makes them easy to identity with.

CLASSICAL/NOBLE ANTIHERO
· *Self-doubting, anxious, fearful*
· *lacks combat skills*
· *Overcomes weakness to beat enemy*
(Jay Gatsby, Bilbo Baggins)

PRAGMATIC ANTIHERO
· *Self-centered*
· *Will act to right wrongs*
· *Does bad things to achieve goals*
(Tyler Durden, Lisbeth Salander)

OUTLAW ANTIHERO
· *Often cynical, alienated*
· *Can be existential, nihilistic*
· *Or conflicted, self-destructive*
(Robin Hood, Bonnie Parker)

RELUCTANT ANTIHERO
· *Forced into action*
· *Finally rises to the occasion*
· *A 'knight in sour armour'*
(Hans Solo, Trinity from Matrix)

UNSCRUPULOUS ANTIHERO
· *Will do whatever it takes*
· *Even if it means hurting others*
· *Does good only if it suits them*
(Becky Sharp, Scarlett O'Hara)

TRAGIC/SYMPATHETIC ANTIHERO
· *Maybe starts on the good side*
· *Actions and values not good*
· *May become a villain by the end*
(Heathcliff, Shylock)

ABOVE: *Six kinds of Antihero.*

VILLAINS
and antivillains

Villains fascinate people. When ambitious and ruthless Lady Macbeth encourages her husband Macbeth to murder King Duncan so they can seize the throne, we recognize her embodiment of the morally reprehensible qualities which are the hallmarks of villains the world over.

Villains exist on a scale from 'bad' to 'evil', and in a narrative can be used to create conflict, provide contrast, examine moral themes, challenge the status quo, and entertain by eliciting strong emotional responses. Opposing a hero protagonist creates tension and excitement, especially if they are supremely cunning like Sherlock Holmes' nemesis Moriarty.

Few people root for reprobates, so even when a villain is the protagonist (like Macbeth, or Raskolnikov in *Crime and Punishment*) readers instead hope for their downfall, while remaining riveted by their wickedness.

Villains are especially potent in plot-led narratives, pushing the action forward and creating tension as they threaten the protagonist(s).

Villains can also educate. By presenting a character who deviates from what is considered "good" or "right," an author can encourage readers to question their own moral or social beliefs.

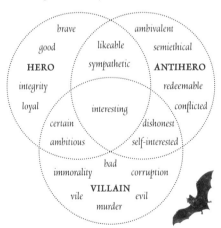

brave · ambivalent
good · likeable · semiethical
HERO · sympathetic · **ANTIHERO**
integrity · redeemable
loyal · interesting · conflicted
certain · dishonest
ambitious · self-interested
bad
immorality · corruption
VILLAIN
vile · evil
murder

Some villains are now understood as **ANTI-VILLAINS**. They are still antagonists, they do the wrong thing, but they are not inherently evil, or even that bad. Inspector Javert in Victor Hugo's *Les Misérables* can be seen in this way, driven by his unwavering dedication to the law.

BEASTS
· *Superhuman strength*
· *Unpredictable nature*
· *Overcome by a deserving hero*
· *Tricked / disabled by hero*
(Minotaur, Goliath, Grendel, Godzilla)

MACHINES
· *Super-human intelligence*
· *Humans not to be trusted*
· *Defy Asimov Laws of Robotics*
· *Total lack of empathy*
(The Machines - War of the Worlds, The Agents - The Matrix, Hal)

MACHIAVELLIAN MASTERMINDS
· *Dubious or no moral compass*
· *Highly intelligent and able*
· *Ruthless in achieving power*
· *Moves covertly, manipulates*
(Iago, Richard III, Lady Macbeth, Uriah Heep, Steerpike)

FEMMES/HOMMES FATALES
· *Compelling and attractive*
· *Overtly sexualised*
· *Acts independently of norms*
· *Very ambitious*
(Salome, Madame de Merteuil, Willoughby, Carmilla, Poison Ivy)

EVIL ITSELF
· *Irredeemably bad*
· *Corrupted / fell from grace*
· *Appearance can be repulsive*
· *Lusts for power and control*
(Satan, Dracula, White Witch, Sauron, Voldemort)

PSYCHOPATHS
· *Lack of empathy*
· *Cunning and manipulative*
· *Lack of remorse*
· *Superficial charm*
(Hannibal Lecter, Tom Ripley, Bellatrix Lestrange)

MOTHER NATURE
· *vs. Human*
· *Has no feeling or morality*
· *Victims die tragically*
· *Humans sometimes to blame*
(The Birds, The Volcano, Winter - Into the Wild, Dust clouds in The Grapes of Wrath)

EXTREME AUTHORITARIANS
· *Represents oppressive regime*
· *Claims to be upholding law*
· *Lack of empathy*
· *Formidable foe*
(Sheriff of Nottingham, Inspector Javert, Big Brother, Nurse Ratched)

ABOVE: Eight types of Villain. Remember, they can occupy multiple categories.

CONFIDANTS & FOILS
and sidekicks and allies

CONFIDANTS are characters with whom another shares their secrets. A staple of Greek and Latin drama, and still widely used, they obviate the need for long monologues or expositions, as they allow access to the thoughts of the main character. They can even act as their conscience.

In a conniving court, Horatio is the only person Hamlet can trust to hear his grievances and tell him the truth. In Ibsen's 1879 play *A Doll's House*, Mrs Linde is confidant and catalyst for protagonist Nora, her own narrative arc preventing the role from feeling contrived. Rupert Everett's character George in the 1990 film *My Best Friend's Wedding* is a classic trusted friend and confidant:

> JULIANNE: *I'm making a big mistake, huh?*
> GEORGE: (shrugs) *Maybe you'll learn something.* (He wraps his hand over hers. She looks down at it.)

The epistolary novels of Samuel Richardson rely on confidants. In *Clarissa* [1748], the protagonist's account of her seduction by the rake Lovelace can only be told to her friend and confidant Anna Howe.

A FOIL is a character whose qualities expose or contrast with those of another. The term comes from Old French, meaning a thin piece of metal that jewels are set on to enhance their brilliance.

In Louisa May Alcott's 1868 novel *Little Women*, the sisters Amy and Beth are foils; one is confident to the point of thoughtlessness, the other kind to the point of selflessness. Sometimes this polarity is the very soul of a novel, such as Hermann Hesse's archetypal tale of two lives:

> It is not our purpose to become each other; it is to recognize each other, to learn to see the other and honor him for what he is: each the other's opposite and complement. Hermann Hesse, Narcissus and Goldmund, 1930

Common traits that are illuminated through foils include:

1. TRUSTING vs. CYNICAL — *Luke Skywalker* vs. *Hans Solo*
2. TYRANNICAL vs. LIBERAL —*Napoleon* vs. *Snowball* Animal Farm
3. IDEALISTIC vs. PRAGMATIC—*Jay Gatsby* vs. *Nick Carraway*
4. CHEERFUL vs. GLOOMY—*Pooh* vs. *Eeyore*
5. DARING vs. COWARDLY—*Scrappy* vs. *Scooby Doo*

A foil may also share traits with another character, but take a different path. In Mary Shelley's 1818 novel *Frankenstein*, the external narrator Robert Walton abandons his desperate quest for the North Pole after witnessing the fate of Frankenstein and realising his own hubris.

SIDEKICKS closely support the principal character (ALLIES give less direct support). Batman has Robin, Robinson Crusoe has Friday, Holmes has Watson, Achilles has Patroclus, Winnie the Pooh has Piglet, and so on. The sidekick may RESCUE (Robin), MEDIATE between a hero and the real world (Watson), HUMANISE heroes who might otherwise seem aloof (Patroclus), PROVIDE MOTIVE to act (e.g. Achilles avenging Patroclus' death), or COMPENSATE for the hero's physical, mental or emotional weaknesses (Friday).

What Kind of Person?
psychology and direct characterisation

Good fiction, like psychology, exposes and unravels a person, delving into

> … *the mysterious aspects of the human soul and its subconscious areas by means of long and detailed journeys* … Ismet Emre

A character's **PERSONALITY** is relatively easy to infer, based on traits like optimism, confidence, humor, and sociability. But psychologist Alex Lickerman describes how this differs from the deeper notion of **CHARACTER**, which takes far longer to figure out:

> It includes traits that reveal themselves only in specific — and often uncommon — circumstances, traits like honesty, virtue, and kindliness.

Of particular interest to psychologists and writers is how a character forms relationships. Their **ATTACHMENT STYLE** can take four forms:

SECURE ATTACHMENT: Jane Eyre forms deep emotional bonds and relies on her partner, Mr. Rochester, for emotional support.

ANXIOUS-AMBIVALENT ATTACHMENT: Anna Karenina constantly seeks reassurance from Count Vronsky, and is fearful of abandonment.

AVOIDANT-DISMISSIVE ATTACHMENT: Jay Gatsby is emotionally distant. He struggles to form close relationships. Wealth hides his insecurities.

DISORGANIZED ATTACHMENT: Hamlet is traumatized. As he struggles to regulate his emotions, confusion and instability colour his relationships.

Describing characters in terms of psychology is often a part of **DIRECT CHARACTERISATION**, contrasting with **INDIRECT** methods (*see pages 38–44*).

Victorian novelists were often masters of the snappy summary:

> *Vanity was the beginning and end of Sir Walter Elliot's character: vanity of person and of situation.* Jane Austen, Persuasion, 1817

Fyodor Dostoevsky's intensely interior writing is similarly psychological:

> *I did not know how to become anything: neither spiteful nor kind, neither a rascal nor an honest man, neither a hero, nor an insect.* Notes from Underground, 1864

Also heading straight to the depths of soul, Pearl Buck, in her 1931 masterpiece *The Good Earth*, describes one of her protagonists, O-lan:

> *But hers was a strange heart, sad in its very nature, and she could never weep and ease it as other women do, for her tears never brought her comfort.*

OPENNESS: how open to new experiences, ideas, and perspectives?

CONSCIENTIOUSNESS: how responsible organized, prudent?

EXTRAVERSION: how outgoing, sociable, and witty?

CHARACTER

AGREEABLENESS: how kind, tolerant, empathetic, and cooperative?

VIRTUES/VICES: how honest, fair, brave, loyal, ethical, patient?

NEUROTICISM: how emotionally unstable, anxious, oversensitive?

EMOTIONAL INTELLIGENCE: how perceptive?

ESSENCE/SOUL integrity

SELF-DISCIPLINE: how able to control sudden impulses?

ASSERTIVENESS: how confident, decisive?

PERSONALITY

RESILIENCE: how able to bounce back?

CREATIVITY: how imaginative, inventive, able to think outside the box?

MOTIVATION & AGENCY
what do they want? why can't they get it?

At the heart of most stories are characters who want something. Sometimes they don't know it. Other times, halfway through, they realize they need something else from what they thought. Either way, they don't always get it at the end. The dramatist Konstantin Stanislavski [1863–1938] wrote:

> *An actor must learn to seek out in every human need, in every human desire, that which is universal, that which is common to all human beings. It is only in this way that he can touch the hearts of his audience, awakening in them a sense of recognition and empathy, and revealing to them the deep and profound truths of the human condition.* An Actor Prepares, 1936

Writers are no different. Want puts a character in motion: in every chapter, behind every scene, driving every line of dialogue. Author David Corbett distinguishes between two types of want: DESIRE and YEARNING:

> *One of the fundamental requirements of a dramatically compelling and thematically unified story is the need to weave together the pursuit of the character's principle goal (Desire) with the fundamental longing it speaks to (Yearning).* The Art of Character, 2013

In Mary Shelley's 1818 novel *Frankenstein*, Victor Frankenstein yearns for scientific glory. This deeper impetus drives his desire to bring his monstrous creation to life, regardless of the costs. In F. Scott Fitzgerald's 1925 novel *The Great Gatsby*, Gatsby yearns for belonging and inclusion in elite society. This drives his desire for wealth and for Daisy Buchanan.

Here are some of the primary goals that motivate many literary characters, good and bad, and the deeper reasons they seek them:

1. LOVE & COMPANIONSHIP: *For meaning, intimacy and acceptance.*

2. SURVIVAL. *Escape: To protect something important.*

3. REVENGE. *Justice: To restore balance to the world.*

4. PERSONAL GROWTH: *To escape illusion and know oneself.*

5. SUCCESS. *In wealth, sport, status, a quest: To be optimal and valued.*

6. REDEMPTION. *Atonement, forgiveness: To heal.*

7. POWER. *Influence, authority: To feel in control.*

Abraham Maslow's 1943 HIERARCHY OF NEEDS (*below*) is a useful model of human behaviour. Many characters pursue their needs on multiple levels simultaneously, and these can often conflict with each other. Such CONTRADICTIONS are a favorite device of both comedy and tragedy writers, the latter perhaps most famously depicted by Shakespeare in *Hamlet*, where the prince is torn between avenging his father's murder and his moral repugnance of the very act of revenge.

Maslow's chart evokes an important question. Does a character actually possess the inner and outer resources, the AGENCY, to get what they need? And if they don't, what needs to happen?

5. SELF-ACTUALIZATION
the desire to become the most that one can be

4. ESTEEM
respect, self-esteem, status, recognition, strength, freedom

3. LOVE AND BELONGING
friendship, intimacy, family, sense of connection

2. SECURITY LEVEL: SAFETY NEEDS
personal security, employment, resources, health, property

1. SURVIVAL LEVEL: PHYSIOLOGICAL NEEDS
air, water, food, shelter, sleep, clothing, reproduction

FRUSTRATION & CONFLICT
what are they up against?

As much as we would like, most of us don't tend to get what we want, at least not immediately. Those who do probably don't get what they really need. In most cases, OBSTACLES stand in the way. Finding out how a character overcomes these obstacles is what keeps readers reading. To paraphrase Hollywood script editor Michael Hague:

> All stories are built on character, desire, and conflict. The protagonist desperately wants or needs something, and must overcome formidable obstacles to achieve it. The greater this conflict, the greater the emotional involvement of readers.

Some obstacles exist OUTSIDE the character. These may be:

1. ENVIRONMENTAL: *Weather, Mountains, Rivers, Walls, Space, Distance.*
2. ANTAGONISTIC: *Villains, Rivals, Adversaries, Authority figures.*
3. SOCIETAL: *Gender, Class, Religion, Law, Politics, Culture.*
4. RESOURCE LIMITATIONS: *Time, Money, Supplies, Personnel.*

In J.R.R. Tolkien's 1937 novel *The Hobbit*, the initially nervous protagonist Bilbo Baggins faces numerous challenges on his unexpected quest, including confronting dangerous creatures, navigating treacherous terrain, and outsmarting terrifying adversaries. In so doing he discovers his own courage, resourcefulness, and the importance of friendship.

Other obstacles exist INSIDE, and are literally part of the character:

1. FEARS: *Insecurity, Self doubt, Cowardice, Indecisiveness, Naivety.*
2. EGO: *Arrogance, Pride, Dishonesty, Greed, Inflexibility, Stubbornness.*

3. NEGATIVE EMOTIONS: *Guilt, Shame, Anger, Disgust, Self-hatred.*
4. OBSESSIONS: *Food, Drink, Sex, Drugs, Wealth, Power, Control.*
5. BELIEFS: *Ethical dilemmas, Prejudices, Skewed values.*

In Harper Lee's 1960 novel *To Kill a Mockingbird*, the protagonist Scout Finch is motivated by her desire for justice and equality, learnt from her father Atticus. However, she faces obstacles in her pursuit of these ideals, including the racism and prejudice of many people in her town.

In Fyodor Dostoevsky's 1866 novel *Crime and Punishment*, law student Raskolnikov commits a double murder for money but then faces feverish inner turmoil and an intense psychological battle with detective Porfiry Petrovich who suspects him of the crime, before he ultimately confesses.

Outer obstacles serve as catalysts for character development and help drive the narrative, creating compelling conflicts and opportunities for growth. Inner obstacles add depth and complexity to characters, making them more relatable and human, while also driving character development and the overall narrative.

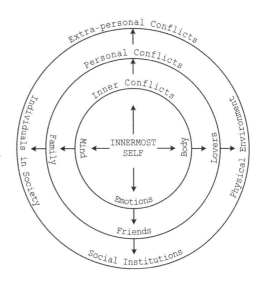

FLAWS, WOUNDS, & SECRETS
why do we care?

No-one is perfect. Perfect characters are remote, boring, and unrealistic. So writers instead create imperfect characters, to foster connections between their creations and their readers, and they do this in three ways:

1. **FLAWS**. Defects make a character more interesting and relatable, building reader *empathy*. A character's FEARS, swollen EGO, negative EMOTIONS, unhealthy OBSESSIONS and rigid BELIEFS (*see p.26–27*) can create obstacles and challenges, leading to poor decisions with consequences. These provide opportunities for self-knowledge, development, and growth.

In Jane Austen's 1813 novel *Pride and Prejudice*, both Elizabeth Bennet and Mr. Darcy are initially proud and prejudiced towards each other. She, from his aloof and arrogant behaviour towards her and her family; he, due to her lower social status and lack of wealth. To realize their love for each other, they must each overcome their own flaws and biases.

	TOO LITTLE	VIRTUE	TOO MUCH
RIGHT: *In Aristotle's Nichomachean Ethics, the vices (character flaws) exist as either deficiencies (too little) or excesses (too much) of the virtues. If you have too little courage, you are a coward, but too much and you are rash. The virtues are achieved by finding the balance between extremes.*	cowardice	COURAGE	recklessness
	stinginess	GENEROSITY	extravagance
	shamelessness	MODESTY	pride
	sloth	AMBITION	greed
	indulgence	SELF CONTROL	insensibility
	paranoia	CONFIDENCE	arrogance
	surliness	FRIENDLINESS	obsequiousness
	deceitfulness	HONESTY	tactlessness
	dullness	WIT	buffoonery

28

2. WOUNDS. A lion is a serious beast. But a lion limping with a thorn in its paw? We immediately feel for it. Wounds build *sympathy* between readers and characters, and provide insight into a character's backstory, motivations, and personality. Wounds can be PHYSICAL (disabling), EMOTIONAL (loss or betrayal), or PSYCHOLOGICAL (trauma).

J. K. Rowling created Harry Potter physically scarred by his enemy Lord Voldemort, emotionally traumatized by the loss of his parents, and psychologically stigmatized for being "the boy who lived". Her next protagonist, detective Cormoran Strike, has half a leg missing, dead and dysfunctional parents, and serious war trauma. In Charlotte Bronte's 1847 novel *Jane Eyre*, her heroine's wound is her upbringing as an orphan, which leaves her feeling isolated and unloved. This wound shapes her personality and decisions throughout the novel.

3. SECRETS. People build shields around their wounds, but they build whole castles around a secret. Together these walls form the mask of a character's ego or persona, maintained by feelings of guilt or shame and the dread of being exposed, then shunned and abandoned. Depicting a character peeling away this mask and finding the courage to be more fully realized is one of the great challenges of good character writing.

In Khaled Hosseini's 2003 novel *The Kite Runner*, young Amir betrays his kite-flying friend and servant Hassan, failing to assist him when he is assaulted by a local bully, pretending he didn't see anything. Unable to confront his guilt and shame, he distances himself from Hassan, and years later moves to America. There he discovers that Hassan was his half-brother, a secret hidden by his father. Returning to Afghanistan to atone for his past actions, he finds that Hassan has died, but his son Sohrab is still alive. Amir achieves redemption by rescuing and adopting Sohrab.

CHARACTER ARCS
feeling the beats

A CHARACTER ARC traces the inner development of a character through the course of a narrative. The term was coined by author and lecturer Michael Hague, who writes that all heroes:

> *… must face the same dilemma: either they drop the identities that keep them feeling safe, or they give up on the things they desperately want. This tug-of-war between living in fear and living courageously is each hero's* INNER CONFLICT. *And the gradual transformation from fear to courage—from identity to essence—is the character's* ARC.

Hague holds that it is character which drives plot, while plot molds character arc. They work in symbiosis. Without the structure of plot—the outer journey—the character cannot have an inner journey (*see pages 24–29, and Hague's six stage structure, opposite*).

There are many types of character arc, but most use a three-act structure:

1. BEGINNING: The character is introduced in their initial state, which may include flaws, weaknesses, or a limited worldview. They may be facing a conflict or challenge that sets the story in motion.

2. MIDDLE: The character undergoes experiences (obstacles, conflicts) that force them to confront their flaws, face their fears or question their beliefs, leading to internal struggles, self-reflection, and action.

3. END: The character reaches a point of resolution or transformation. They have learned valuable lessons, overcome their internal or external challenges, and evolved. Their beliefs, values, or behavior may have changed, allowing them to achieve their goals or find fulfillment.

BEATS, originally a filmmaking term describing a moment of change that propels a narrative forward, can be seen as key moments that impact the inner journey. In a three act structure, a protagonist may have, say, three major beats in each act (such as a moment of realization, a setback and a reward/conflict) while antagonists, deuteragonists, and tritagonists may have one or two. Significant beats at the end of each act will be TURNING POINTS, both for the plot and the characterisation.

There are many tools to help develop arcs. Elizabeth Boyle's DREAM tool asks a character to: Deny, Resist, Explore, Accept and Manifest, as in: [D] *Never!* [R] *Go away!* [E] *Okay, dinner!* [A] *I'm in love!* [M] *Let's move in together!* Or there's the P-SQUARE tool: What [P]romises does the writer make? How [P]roactive is the character? What is the [P]rogress? What is the [P]ayoff?

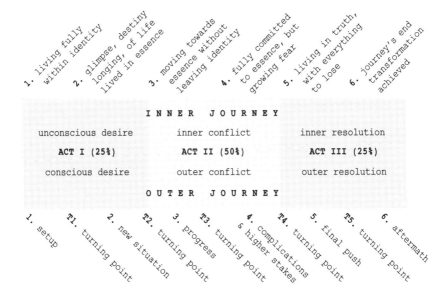

1. living fully within identity
2. glimpse, destiny longing, of life lived in essence
3. moving towards essence without leaving identity
4. fully committed to essence, but growing fear
5. living in truth, with everything to lose
6. journey's end transformation achieved

INNER JOURNEY		
unconscious desire	inner conflict	inner resolution
ACT I (25%)	**ACT II (50%)**	**ACT III (25%)**
conscious desire	outer conflict	outer resolution
OUTER JOURNEY		

1. setup
T1. turning point
2. new situation
T2. turning point
3. progress
T3. turning point
4. complications & higher stakes
T4. turning point
5. final push
T5. turning point
6. aftermath

POSITIVE GROWTH ARCS
change is good

The **POSITIVE CHANGE ARC** does what it says on the tin. By the end of their arc, the character is radically transformed in some positive way. They have been on a difficult journey and come out the other side better for it.

As the arc commences, a character's beliefs or values are challenged or contradicted via a series of beats. The character resists (change is tough), and they may progress slightly, but also regress to former habits. By the end of the narrative, though, they emerge with a different mindset.

Scrooge from *A Christmas Carol*, is a seminal example. The character of Guy Montag in Ray Bradbury's *Fahrenheit 451* transforms from a book burning state enforcer into a fugitive protector of literature after a dawning realization that he has been fighting on the wrong side.

Chief Bromden in *One Flew Over the Cuckoo's Nest* is a transformative deuteragonist; initially a mute figure conforming to asylum rules, he gains courage and freedom, spurred into action by Randall's zest for life.

In the **GROWTH ARC**, a character does not undergo the about-face alteration seen above, but does emerge a wiser version of their original self.

In Sylvia Plath's semi-autobiographical novel *The Bell Jar*, an array of traumatic experiences result in Esther Greenwood moving to a psychiatric institution. The story closes with Esther emerging from under the metaphorical 'bell jar' of her depression, which still 'hovers' just above her head, but she is more mature and logical than the panicked person she was. Susanna Kaysen's 1993 novel *Girl, Interrupted* follows a similar trajectory.

In JB Priestley's 1945 morality play *An Inspector Calls*, Sheila Birling undergoes significant maturation in the course of a single evening. Starting out as a rather silly and spoiled girl, by the finale she is the only one willing to recognise the family's culpability in the suicide of Eva Smith.

Positive growth arcs reflect the twelve-stage process of the Hero's Journey (*below*). Or they can be understood in seven stages:

1. INITIAL STATE. *Flaws, issues, weaknesses, negativity, skewed worldview.*
2. CATALYST. *Something happens, challenges beliefs, highlights flaws*
3. RESISTANCE AND STRUGGLE. *Internal and external obstacles to change.*
4. SELF-REFLECTION AND LEARNING. *New insights, recognition, mentors.*
5. ACTION AND TRANSFORMATION. *Action to change and address issues.*
6. CLIMAX AND RESOLUTION. *Ultimate test, application of lessons & growth.*
7. NEW STATE. *New strength, virtues, positivity. (Some) flaws overcome.*

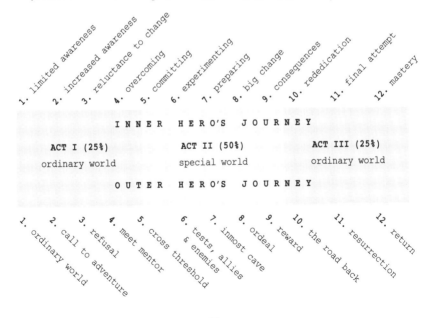

1. limited awareness
2. increased awareness
3. reluctance to change
4. overcoming
5. committing
6. experimenting
7. preparing
8. big change
9. consequences
10. rededication
11. final attempt
12. mastery

INNER HERO'S JOURNEY

ACT I (25%)
ordinary world

ACT II (50%)
special world

ACT III (25%)
ordinary world

OUTER HERO'S JOURNEY

1. ordinary world
2. call to adventure
3. refusal
4. meet mentor
5. cross threshold
6. tests, allies & enemies
7. inmost cave
8. ordeal
9. reward
10. the road back
11. resurrection
12. return

DECLINING ARCS
downhill all the way

The **DECLINE ARC** (or negative change arc) follows a character from success to failure and even death. In these arcs, a staple of antagonists, antiheroes, and tragic dramas, characters undergo a reversal of fortune (Aristotle's **PERIPETEIA**), often due to their own errors (**HAMARTIA**).

The conniving antagonist Sir Percival Glyde in Wilkie Collins' 1859 novel *The Woman in White* sets out as the fiancé of beautiful heiress Laura Fairlie. Once married, however, he becomes cruel, and in a feverish haste to hide his dark history he burns to death in a church fire of his own creation. Ambrosio, the eponymous monk of Matthew Lewis' 1796 Gothic novel, begins the narrative in a near demigod state of holiness:

> *Tranquillity reigned upon his smooth unwrinkled forehead; and Content, expressed upon every feature, seemed to announce the Man equally unacquainted with cares and crimes.* Matthew Lewis, Ambrosio, 1796

He swiftly declines, committing numerous heinous crimes. After one Faustian bargain too many, he is dashed onto rocks by familiars of the devil.

Downfall does not always mean death. George, in John Steinbeck's 1937 novella *Of Mice and Men*, begins full of hope on a new ranch, but ends up a lone itinerant worker in a brutal world. Sometimes the downfall is caused by factors outside the character's control, so they are more victim than creator of their own fates. An example is the declining character arc of Piggy, in William Golding's 1954 novel *The Lord of the Flies*, which mirrors the deteriorating morality of the boys on the island.

There are many types of negative character arcs (*see examples opposite*).

		DISILLUSIONMENT ARC	FALL ARC	CORRUPTION ARC	FLAT ARC
SETUP	1%	they believe in the comfortable lie	they totally believe in the lie	they fully understand the truth	they believe in truth in a lie-soaked world
INCITING	12%	a first hint that the lie may not be true	a first hint that the lie will not suffice	their first taste of the tempting lie	they have to use truth to oppose the lie
PLOT PT 1	25%	they suddenly experience the stark truth	they wonder about truth, but cling to the lie	they enter the entrancing world of the lie	the world pushes back to impose the lie on them
PINCH PT 1	38%	they are punished for using the lie	they try to discover the truth, with limited success	they are torn between truth and the lie	they are unsure if truth can ever defeat the lie
PLOT PT 2	50%	they are forced to face the truth, but do not like it	they glimpse truth, but reject it, and choose a worse lie	they embrace the lie, but do not reject the truth	they prove the power of the truth to the world
PINCH PT 2	62%	they dislike both the old lie and the new truth	worse lie works, but is corrosive, destructive	they reject the sacrifice demanded by truth	servants of the lie now fight back
PLOT PT 3	75%	they accept that the old lie is now gone	they fail to attain their goal, or desire	they fully embrace the lie, and reject the truth	appallingly, the lie seems to triumph
CLIMAX	88%	they wield a dark new truth in final confrontation	a last attempt to attain their goal or desire	their final attempt to gain their goal or desire	final showdown between truth and the lie
PEAK	98%	they now fully acknowledge the tragic truth	they fail completely, and are destroyed	they utterly fail, and lose everything	wonderfully, truth defeats the lie
RESOLUTION	100%	disillusioned with new truth	aftermath, postscript	aftermath, postscript	new world of truth

ACT I — SETUP to PLOT PT 1
ACT II — PINCH PT 1 to PLOT PT 3
ACT III — CLIMAX to RESOLUTION

ABOVE: Negative change arcs vs. a flat arc. Negative change arcs are about failure and the destruction of the self. The flat arc is about saving others. After K. M. Weiland.

35

INVENTING CHARACTER
what's their name?

How do you develop convincing characters? How do you move from fledgling ideas to compelling characters with personalities of their own?

To begin, consider following some tried and tested techniques:

OBSERVE people that you encounter: their stories, opinions, and mannerisms, the way they speak, walk, dress, and drink a glass of water. They are all potential *characters (see Theophrastus' examples p.vi).*

KEEP A NOTEBOOK of these character details: The father who walks too fast for his daughter every day on the way to school. The taxi driver who was once a history teacher in another country.

READ and reread re-existing works to see what is already out there:

> *A painter who wants to paint a tree needs to do two things: look at trees and look at paintings of trees. The first task shows what trees are like, the second shows the possibilities of the medium.* Andrew Miller

INVENT from the caverns of your own imagination. Miller again:

> *The great majority of my characters — and I would guess this is true for most writers of fiction — are "inventions". They emerge, quickly or slowly, shyly or boisterously, in the writing. They are members of that shifting population of men, women and children (not to mention cats, horses, etc.) who inhabit our inner worlds.*

Over the pages which follow we will learn how to show, build and animate a complex character, progressing to a detailed CHARACTER PROFILE (*see pages 54–58*), with their idiosyncratic characteristics and backstory.

But first, we need to give them a name.

WHAT'S IN A NAME? Quite a lot! Many writers even change their names to create a new PERSONA. Eric Blair wrote under the PSEUDONYM George Orwell. Portuguese writer Fernando Pessoa went further, a *nomadic wanderer through [his own] consciousness* he *broke his soul into different persons* to create multiple characters—HETERONYMS—to do his *actual* writing.

Familiar names, news sources, or the phone book are good sources for creating a relative every[wo]man. Rollo Martins and Harry Lime from Graham Greene's *The Third Man* are people you might bump into on the street. Patricia Highsmith's Tom Ripley has a disarmingly everyday name which belies a very complex individual.

Names can be indicative of ethnic background and social class: Vito Corleone in *Godfather*, the rural youth Tom Jones, aristocratic Dorian Gray, or George Eliot's upper-middle class Dorothea Brooke.

Consider also the PHONOLOGY and EUPHONICS of character names:

> *Names with soft consonants such as [m], [n], and [l] tend to sound nicer than names with hard consonants such as [k] and [g]. Imagine two alien races — the Lamonians and Grataks. Which sounds friendlier?* D. Crystal, *Little Book of Language*

CHARACTONYMS (or EUONYMS) indicate a name suited to the nature or occupation of a character. Dickens was a master of this technique. Think of the beautiful and innocent Rosa Bud or the prickly lawyer Mr Jaggers. Or consider Trollope's heroine Eleanor Bold, and his villain Mr Slope.

Mr. Turveydrop
'Bleak House'

Dolly Varden
'Barnaby Rudge'

Mr. Pecksniff
'Martin Chuzzlewit'

The Artful Dodger
'Oliver Twist'

Scrooge
'A Christmas Carol'

Fanny Squeers
'Nicholas Nickleby'

Mr. Stryver
'A Tale of Two Cities'

APPEARANCE
what do they look like?

The art of representing a character in narrative and dramatic works is known as **CHARACTERISATION**. What they look like (*this page*), where they live and work (*p.40*), how they act and react (*p.42*), think (*p.44*) and speak (*pp.46–53*), are all ways of conveying character.

Character **MANNERISMS** can instantly conjure up a mental picture:

> *She was fifteen and she had a quick, nervous giggling habit of craning her neck to glance into mirrors or checking other people's faces to make sure her own was all right.* Joyce Carol Oates, *Where Are You Going, Where Have You Been?* 1966.

A classic study in **BODY LANGUAGE** can be found in Dickens' *David Copperfield* and the Machiavellian character of Uriah Heep:

> *It was no fancy of mine about his hands, I observed; for he frequently ground the palms against each other as if to squeeze them dry and warm, besides often wiping them, in a stealthy way, on his pocket-handkerchief.*

A child crossing a room, may *walk, stomp, skip, scuttle, dawdle* or *hurry*, depending on personality or mood. **EYES** can say everything. Catherine Earnshaw in *Wuthering Heights* has eyes which *are dark and stormy, like the sea on a cloudy day.* Thackeray's *Vanity Fair* antihero Becky Sharp is:

> *…small and slight in person; pale, sandy-haired, and with eyes habitually cast down: when they looked up they were very large, odd, and attractive.*

FACES and **SMILES** are equally revealing, though not always welcome:

> *My brother Ben's face, thought Eugene, is like a piece of slightly yellow ivory; his high white head is knotted fiercely by his old man's scowl; his mouth is like*

a knife, his smile the flicker of light across a blade. T. Wolfe. Look Homeward, Angel

Jay Gatsby, on the other hand, is someone that you want to meet. He has:

> *one of those rare smiles with a quality of eternal reassurance in it, that you may come across four or five times in life.*

Mark Twain is a master of the unsettling 'look'. Here he describes Huck Finn's father with poetic simplicity:

> *He was most fifty, and he looked it. His hair was long and tangled and greasy, and hung down, and you could see his eyes shining through like he was behind vines.*

The CLOTHES a character wears can project personality and professional status. Here is an unselfconscious man, confident in his social position:

> *… most of the men were dressed in dinner jackets with black ties, and some even wore frock coats. Only the most sophisticated, Dr. Urbino among them, wore their ordinary clothes.* Gabriel Garcia Marquez, Love in the Time of Cholera, 1985.

Kate Chopin uses clothing to establish foiling between two female characters Edna and Madame Ratignolle in her 1899 novel *The Awakening*. Virginia Woolf was fascinated by 'frock consciousness'. Her 1928 novel *Orlando* uses clothing as a recurring trope to explore gender roles; we learn that: *clothes wear us, not we them* and that *They change our view of the world and the world's view of us.* However, too much detail is not always convincing: Stephen King lets the reader's imagination do most of the work:

> *I'd rather let the reader supply the faces, the builds, and the clothing as well. If I tell you that Carrie White is a high school outcast with a bad complexion and a fashion-victim wardrobe, I think you can do the rest, can't you?*

Environment
where do they live?

How characters choose, adapt, and interact with their physical surroundings says a lot about who they are and how they wish to be seen.

Homes are especially telling. Wuthering Heights, abode of gruff antihero Heathcliff, is *grotesque, with strong, narrow windows... deeply set in the wall*. Whereas Thrushcross Grange, where well-mannered, graceful Edgar Linton lives:

> *is elegant and comfortable... a splendid place carpeted with crimson, and crimson covered chairs and tables, and a pure white ceiling bordered by gold.*

Dickens, describing the decaying Miss Havisham's mothballed Satis House in *Great Expectations* also conflates persona and place:

> *It was spacious and I dare say had once been handsome, but every discernible thing in it was covered with dust and mold, and dropping to pieces ...*

The noveau-riche facade of Jay Gatsby's sprawling long Island mansion is no less revealing, but for very different reasons. He inhabits:

> *... a factual imitation of some Hotel de Ville in Normandy, with a tower on one side, spanking new under a thin beard of raw ivy, and a marble swimming pool, and more than forty acres of lawn and garden ...*

Likewise, intimate spaces can speak volumes, be it a cosy Hobbit house with *lots and lots of pegs for hats and coats, the hobbit was fond of visitors*, or a bedroom, such as Father Zossima's in *The Brothers Karamazov*:

> *... a little room furnished with the bare necessities. There was a narrow iron bedstead, with a strip of felt for a mattress. In the corner, under the ikons, was a reading-desk with a cross and the Gospel lying on it.*

Jack Kerouac's characters occupy spaces which reflect the values, lifestyles and personalities of the Beat Generation:

> *Sean's house had woven straw mats on the floor and there too when you came in you were required to take off your shoes. He had lots of books and the only extravagance was a hi-fi set so he could play his fine collection of Indian records and Flamenco records and jazz. He even had Chinese and Japanese records.* The Dharma Bums, 1958.

How characters treat animals and how they appreciate nature also reveals much about their inner landscape and worldview:

> *Look at the rain long enough, with no thoughts in your head, and you gradually feel your body falling loose, shaking free of the world of reality. Rain has the power to hypnotize.* Hajimi in South of the Border, West of the Sun, Haruki Murakami, 1992

Some character's lives are intimately bonded with land and elements:

> *When June was half gone, the big clouds moved up out of Texas and the Gulf, high heavy clouds, rain-heads. The men in the fields looked up at the clouds and sniffed at them and held wet fingers up to sense the wind.* J. Steinbeck, The Grapes of Wrath, 1939.

Setting is especially important in television and film, where time constraints require each shot to tell a thousand words. Nuanced details, such as a family photograph on an office desk, children's toys, furniture, artworks, or a stack of dishes, all hint at the backstory, personality, and inner life of a character.

ACTION & REACTION
what are they like?

Much can be inferred about a character through their physical actions and emotional reactions. Aristotle held that if a character is unpredictable they should be *consistently inconsistent* in their behaviour.

A modern master of deeply revealing routine is Haruki Murakami. Here is protagonist Toru from his 1994 novel *The Wind-Up Bird Chronicle*:

> When the phone rang I was in the kitchen, boiling a potful of spaghetti and whistling along with an FM broadcast of the overture to Rossini's 'The Thieving Magpie,' which has to be the perfect music for cooking pasta.

His Doweger from IQ84 eats small portions of French-influenced lunches like *boiled white asparagus, salad Niçoise, and a crabmeat omelet* and takes her tea like *a fairy deep in the forest sipping a life-giving morning dew.*

> You get the sense from her diet and table manners not only that she's well-bred and refined, but almost enlightened. Elaheh Nozari

John Steinbeck uses small details built up over time to portray the socioeconomic realities of his everyman characters:

> Joad took a quick drink from the flask. He dragged the last smoke from his raveling cigarette and then, with callused thumb and forefinger, crushed out the glowing end. He rubbed the butt to a pulp and put it out the window, letting the breeze suck it from his fingers. John Steinbeck, *The Grapes of Wrath*, 1939.

Sometimes a character describes themselves for us, as with Captain Nemo's angry reaction to Professor Pierre Aronnax, the narrator in Jules Verne's 1870 novel *Twenty Thousand Leagues Under the Sea*:

"Professor," replied the commander, quickly, "I am not what you call a civilized man! I have done with society entirely, for reasons which I alone have the right of appreciating. I do not, therefore, obey its laws, and I desire you never to allude to them before me again!"

This was said plainly. A flash of anger and disdain kindled in the eyes of the Unknown, and I had a glimpse of a terrible past in the life of this man.

In Leo Tolstoy's 1877 novel *Anna Karenina*, landowner Konstantin Levin both acts on and reacts against his love for Kitty:

After spending two months in Moscow, as if in a daze, seeing Kitty almost every day in society, which he began to frequent in order to meet her, Levin suddenly decided that it could not be and left for the country. Levin's conviction that it could not be rested on the idea that in the eyes of her relatives he was an unprofitable, unworthy match for the charming Kitty, and that Kitty could not love him.

In Vikram Seth's 1993 novel *A Suitable Boy*, 19-year-old Lata's initial reaction to charming Maan says much about her:

'I see you're enjoying yourself,' said Maan to her in English.

Lata was struck shy, as she sometimes was with strangers, especially those who smiled as boldly as Maan. Let him do the smiling for both of us, she thought.

'Yes,' she said simply, her eyes resting on his face for just a second.

Of course, more clear-cut actions and reactions also work well too (*right*).

THOUGHTS
what are they thinking?

Revealing what a character is thinking is a defining feature of literary characterization; authors have free reign to depict mental landscapes, conveying unspoken observations and a myriad of inner feelings.

In *Brave New World* expressions of individuality are not tolerated, but Bernard's dissenting introspection foreshadows his external rebellion:

> "Didn't you think it was wonderful?" she insisted, looking into Bernard's face with those supernaturally shining eyes.
> "Yes, I thought it was wonderful," he lied and looked away; the sight of her transfigured face was at once an accusation and an ironical reminder of his own separateness. Aldous Huxley, Brave New World, 1932.

Most thoughts are not shared. They are private musings, egodystonic intrusions (unwanted thoughts), speculations and shallow observations:

> Watching Portia she thought, is she a snake, or a rabbit? At all events, she thought, hardening, she has her own fun. Elizabeth Bowen, Anna in The Death of the Heart, 1938.

Thoughts can be used to hint at a character's backstory:

> Narcissus pondered a great deal about his friend... Was it not strange and suspicious? Whenever Goldmund told a story about a trout he had caught as a boy, when he described a butterfly, imitated the call of a bird, spoke of a friend, a dog, a beggar, he created a vivid picture. Whenever he spoke of his father, one saw nothing. Hermann Hesse, Narcissus and Goldman, 1930

Show their blindness to obvious facts:

> He thought it very discouraging that his wife, who was the sole object of his

existence, evinced so little interest in things which concerned him, and valued so little his conversation. Léonce Pontellier in The Awakening. Kate Chopin.

Or reveal their tensions and suppressed emotions:

I kept thinking the waiter might commit an indiscretion and say: 'Will Mademoiselle be dining with Monsieur tonight as usual?' I felt a little sick whenever he came near the table, but he said nothing. Daphne du Maurier, Rebecca.

By following train of thought, we get beneath the surface of a character:

Rottcodd was longing to get back to his hammock and enjoy the luxury of being quite alone again, but his eye travelled even more speedily towards the visitor's face when he heard the remark. Mr. Flay had said that he saw what Rottcodd had meant. Had he really? Very interesting. What, by the way, had he meant? What precisely was it that Mr. Flay had seen? Mervyn Peake, Titus Groan, 1946.

Much can also be inferred through the nuances of tortured self-justification:

At moments he felt he was raving. He sank into a state of feverish excitement. 'The old woman is of no consequence,' he thought, hotly and incoherently. 'The old woman was a mistake perhaps, but she is not what matters! The old woman was only an illness.... I was in a hurry to overstep.... I didn't kill a human being, but a principle! Fyodor Dostoevsky, Crime and Punishment, 1866.

Mind can be the crucible of all experience. Stream of consciousness writers like Virginia Wolf and James Joyce immerse us in uncensored thoughts. Who am I? Why am I? What I am doing? All merge in a tumult:

The world wavered and quivered and threatened to burst into flames. It is I who am blocking the way, he thought. Was he not being looked at and pointed at; was he not weighted there, rooted to the pavement, for a purpose? But for what purpose? Septimus, in Mrs Dalloway, Virginia Woolf, 1925.

DIALOGUE
what do they say?

First consider whether you *need* dialogue at all? As Alfred Hitchcock once said: *Drama is life with the boring bits cut out.* Many modern writers abide by the THREE BEAT RULE, to never let a speaker go past three DIALOGUE BEATS (effectively three sentences) before an ACTION BEAT.

> *"What would happen," I said, "if a mortal saw you in your fullest glory?"* (1)
> *"He would be burned to ash in a second."* (2)
> *"What if a mortal saw me?"* (3)
> *My father smiled. I listened to the draught pieces moving, the familiar rasp of marble against wood. (action beat)* Madeline Miller, *Circe*, 2019

DIALOGUE TAGS frame and identify speech, the 'he said', 'she whispered', 'I asked' of dialogue. How best to use them is debated. One approach is to keep it functional and stick mostly to 'said', or different tense forms of it:

> *['Said'] is a convention so firmly established that readers for the most part do not even see it. This helps to make the dialogue realistic by keeping its superstructure invisible.* Mittelmark & Newman, *How Not to Write a Novel*, 2008.

Placement of dialogue tags can convey added meaning—they do not have to be at the beginnings and ends of utterances. There is also much to be said for keeping their use to a minimum, as Hemingway liked to do:

> *"Do you know any dirt?" I asked.*
> *"No."*
> *"None of your exalted connections getting divorces?"*
> *"No; listen, Jake. If I handled both our expenses, would you go to South America with me?"* Ernest Hemingway, *The Sun Also Rises*, 1926.

It is often wise to avoid *telling* how a speaker is feeling (the 'no adverb rule'), and instead *show* it. Compare these two styles:

> "I think he's outside," Alex whispered fearfully.

> Her eyes widened, her finger flew to her lips. "I think he's outside," Alex whispered.

Stephen King cautions against *shooting the attribution verb full of steroids* to make up for missing adverbs: the *Jekyll grated, Shayna gasped or Bill bellowed* of pulp fiction novels. Whatever rules you abide by, or break, remember that:

> Story time is compressed time. An entire life can be told in the space of just ninety minutes and still somehow feel complete. It's this compression that's the secret of arresting dialogue. Will Storr, The Science of Storytelling, 2019.

Rules for PUNCTUATION in dialogue exist to help both writer and reader. They can be bent for stylistic or dialectical purposes, but all writers should know the standard form. Whatever you do, be consistent. This extract from P G Wodehouse contains *nearly* everything you need to know:

> "Hallo, Mabel!" he said, with a sort of gulp.
> "Hallo!" said the girl.
> "Mabel," said Bingo, "this is Bertie Wooster, a pal of mine."
> "Pleased to meet you," she said. "Nice morning."
> "Fine," I said.
> "You see I'm wearing the tie," said Bingo.
> "It suits you beautiful," said the girl. P G Wodehouse, Jeeves in the Springtime, 1921

Note the speech marks around direct speech (either single or double), a comma after a tag that interrupts speech (line 3), how punctuation is always added before closing speech marks, how new speakers appear on a new line, and that continued dialogue need not begin with a capital letter (line 3).

DIALECT
how do they say it?

DIALECT, denoting regional and social origin, and IDIOLECT, a single individual's idiosyncratic use of language, are important features of characterization. Both combine ACCENT, GRAMMAR and LEXIS (vocabulary). To convey either, and capture the particular accent, the dialogue is often written partially phonetically:

… some wise guy dat I neveh seen befoeh pipes up … "Yuh change to duh West End line at Toity-sixt". Thomas Wolfe, *Only the Dead Know Brooklyn*, 1935.

In *The Colour Purple*, Alice Walker manipulates the grammar of the character Celie to reflect her heritage and rural Georgia accent:

"I think she mine. My heart say she mine. But I don't know she mine. If she mine, her name Olivia. I embroder Olivia in the seat of all her daidies."

Often the words themselves are revealing. Only a privileged, precocious little girl (in this case the titular young Sara) could use this lexicon:

"Well, papa," she said softly, "if we are here I suppose we must be resigned".

Frances Hodgson Burnett, *A Little Princess*, 1905

Dialectal features can highlight social differences *between* characters:

LIZA: I ain't got no mother. Her that turned me out was my sixth stepmother. But I done without them. And I'm a good girl, I am.
HIGGINS: Very well, then, what on earth is all this fuss about? The girl doesn't belong to anybody — is no use to anybody but me. G.B. Shaw, *Pygmalion*.

The plot of Pygmalion revolves around Professor Higgins' attempts to teach Eliza (a poor flower seller) to talk correctly, with the accent of a lady. Much can be inferred from this exchange about Eliza's potentially fragile inner world, in contrast to Higgin's seemingly unemotional command of himself and his planned human experiment. Two very different characters laid bare in four lines of dialogue.

Often, less is more—what is *not* said can carry the greater weight. In Edith Wharton's 1920 novel *Age of Innocence*, high society characters like Lawrence Lefferts mask deceit with conventions of gender and class:

> "I say, old chap: do you mind just letting it be understood that I'm dining with you at the club tomorrow night? Thanks so much, you old brick!"

For his novel *Riddley Walker*, author Russell Hoban had to imagine what the English language might be like centuries in the future:

> She sung that in my ear then we freshent the Luck up there on top of the gate house. She wer the oldes in our crowd but her voyce wernt old. It made the res of her seam yung for a littl. Russell Hoban, Riddley Walker, 1980

Note that too heavy a dialect can be cumbersome to read:

> 'T' maister's down i' t' fowld. Go round by th' end o' t' laith, if ye went to spake to him. Joseph, in Emily Brontë's, Wuthering Heights, 1847.

An absence of local dialect can be clinical. In George Orwell's dystopian novel *1984*, the ruling Party has invented "Newspeak," a stripped-down authoritarian version of English designed to manipulate and control the population by limiting the range of thought to prevent dissent:

> "Don't you see that the whole aim of Newspeak is to narrow the range of thought? In the end we shall make thoughtcrime literally impossible, because there will be no words in which to express it." George Orwell, "1984", 1949.

REAL SPEECH
how convergent are they?

The way people converse (and think) in creative works is mostly **STYLISED**. Transcribing actual speech can reveal a lot about **REAL** dialogue:

FAMILY CHAT (15 SECONDS)

SMJ: *erm lounge as well (.) sorry*

JM: *Yeah // was a right*

SMJ: *// did you notice //*

JM: *// yeah it was a right old mess [inaudible]*

MMJ: *What you doing?*

SMJ: *Did you notice how we've painted it?*

EJ: *// Bye Mark, bye Darcie, bye mum //*

JM: *// no I must admit I didn't // (2) really notice*

MMJ: *// Ta-ra*

SMJ: *[laughs]*

OMJ: *Ra-ra-raaa-ra*

DMJ: *Mummy have you seen (.) Oti's [inaudible]*

(*//*) indicates interruption; (.) indicates pause; (2) indicates 2 second pause.

Actual speech, as you can see, is typified by interruptions, false starts, pauses, overlaps, tangents, repetition, backchanneling (responding with 'yes' 'uh-huh' 'oh dear' etc), non-verbal features like laughing, and so on. **PARALINGUISTIC** features (body language), **DEIXIS** (verbal pointing, e.g. what's that?) and **PROSODY** (stress and intonation) are also important.

Linguist Paul Grice outlines four maxims that we intuitively stick to in order to make conversations work: **QUANTITY**—not saying too much or too little; **QUALITY**—saying the truth; **RELEVANCE**—staying on topic; **MANNER**—speaking in a coherent structure. As seen above, we do not stick to these rules when engaged in casual conversation, but in formal ones we at least try. In some contexts we 'flout' the maxims, e.g. if someone we know is upset they can flout the maxim of quantity.

We often change our language according to better fit the context of the conversation and the person or group of people we are speaking to. Linguist Howard Giles outlines four ways this can manifest:

UPWARDS CONVERGENCE: *A speaker makes themselves sound more formal.*
DOWNWARDS CONVERGENCE: *They sound more colloquial than usual.*
MUTUAL CONVERGENCE: *Speakers become similar to one another.*
DIVERGENCE: *One or both speakers emphasize their different manners of speaking. Can be an exercise in asserting power.*

Different ways of talking have different social values at different points. OVERT PRESTIGE comes from talking 'properly', valued by the upper echelons of society, signalling good education and reliability:

I want to be a lady in a flower shop stead of selling at the corner of Tottenham Court Road. But they won't take me unless I can talk more genteel. Pygmalion

COVERT PRESTIGE comes from talking in a non-standard, linguistically rebellious way. It usually requires downwards convergence. SOCIOLECTS are dialects which emerge between speakers whose language converges to demonstrate shared identity or social attitude.

Gautam Malkani's 2006 novel *Londonstani* captures the language of Pakistani teenagers embroiled in gang culture:

*U hear me, blud? Where we meeting Davinder?
I already told u, u thick khota: outside Nando's,
innit, goes Hardjit.... I also told'chyu we had 2 call
Davinder b4 we left dis place, innit, so any u chiefs
know his mobile?*

NATURAL OR REAL?
how natural does it sound?

Real life spoken language is messy and hard to follow on the page. Your challenge as a writer is to stylise speech that sounds convincing, while at the same time allowing it to drive characterization and narrative.

In the extract below from Ottessa Moshfegh's 2018 novel *My Year of Rest and Relaxation* the protagonist is in conversation with her new therapist:

> "I'm very good with insurance companies," she said matter-of-factly. "I know how to play into their little games. Are you sleeping at *all*?"
>
> "Barely," I said.
>
> "Any dreams?"
>
> "Only nightmares."
>
> "I figured. Sleep is key. Most people need upwards of fourteen hours or so. The modern age has forced us to live unnatural lives. Busy, busy, busy. Go, go, go. You probably work too much." She scribbled for a while on her pad.
>
> "*Mirth*," Dr. Tuttle said. "I like it better than joy. *Happiness* isn't a word I like to use in here. It's very arresting, happiness. You should know that I'm someone who appreciates the subtleties of human experience. Being well rested is a precondition, of course. Do you know what *mirth* means? M-I-R-T-H?"

Dr Tuttle's characterization is partly built on her habit of emphasizing important words; she is fond of COLLOQUIALISMS ('I figured'), and repetition. Her occupation is suggested by niche vocabulary ('a precondition'). In this semi-formal situation, our speakers abide by the maxim of relevance, but Dr Tuttle's more powerful position allows her longer speeches, flouting the maxim of quantity. These features are typical of natural speech but the language is stylized: no pauses, false starts, interruptions etc (*see page 50*).

The schools of **NATURALISM** and **REALISM**, which emerged in the 19th century, saw writers and dramatists move away from **MELODRAMA** towards more relatable characters and themes. Henrik Ibsen is considered the father of the Realist movement. His character Nora is typical of the genre; she is inwardly motivated, independent of thought. There is still stylization in the orderly and selective flow of words, but pause, repetition and exclamation bring her closer to how the audience themselves would speak.

> For eight years I've been waiting patiently; I knew, of course, that such things don't happen every day. Then, when this trouble came to me - I thought to myself; Now! Now the wonderful thing will happen! Henrik Ibsen, A Doll's House, 1879.

Naturalist dramas tend to include speech which is a step closer to the natural. Here is Tusenbach in *The Three Sisters* by Anton Chekhov:

> Not only in two or three centuries but in a million years, life will be just the same; life does not change, it keeps on following its own laws which do not concern us, or which, anyway, we'll never find out. Migrant birds, cranes for example, fly backwards and forwards, and whatever ideas, great or small, stray through their minds, they still go on flying just the same... Anton Chekhov, The Three Sisters, 1901.

With a repetitive and uneven flow of tumbling thoughts, the words are closer to real-life conversation. We can see the legacy of these styles in film scripts, such as the 1976 film *Network*:

> Well, I'm not gonna leave you alone. I want you to get MAD! I don't want you to protest. I don't want you to riot — I don't want you to write to your congressman, because I wouldn't know what to tell you to write. I don't know what to do about the depression and the inflation and the Russians and the crime in the street. All I know is that first you've got to get mad. (shouting) You've got to say: 'I'm a human being, god-dammit! My life has value! Paddy Chayefsky, Network, 1976.

Summary & Sketches
who are they?

Authors often outline their characters for their readers within a SUMMARY, embedded in the narrative. Conan Doyle has Dr. Watson cleverly write down a quick summary sketch of Sherlock Holmes at their very first meeting in his 1887 novel *A Study in Scarlett*:

SHERLOCK HOLMES—*his limits*
1. *Knowledge of Literature.—Nil.*
2. *Philosophy.—Nil.*
3. *Astronomy.—Nil.*
4. *Politics.—Feeble.*
5. *Botany.—Variable. Well up in belladonna, opium, and poisons generally. Knows nothing of practical gardening.*
6. *Knowledge of Geology.—Practical, but limited. Tells at a glance different soils from each other. After walks has shown me splashes upon his trousers, and told me by their colour and consistence in what part of London he had received them.*
7. *Knowledge of Chemistry.—Profound.*
8. *Anatomy.—Accurate, but unsystematic.*
9. *Sensational Literature.—Immense. He appears to know every detail of every horror perpetrated in the century.*
10. *Plays the violin well.*
11. *Is an expert singlestick player, boxer, and swordsman.*
12. *Has a good practical knowledge of British law.*

Here is a classic summary from *Don Quixote* by Miguel de Cervantes. We find out Don Quixote's work and leisure habits, hobbies and passions, and the consequences of pursuing these—his obsession, illness and madness. Cervantes goes on with it for several pages:

This gentleman, in the times when he had nothing to do—as was the case for most of the year—gave himself up to the reading of books of knight errantry;

which he loved and enjoyed so much that he almost entirely forgot his hunting, and even the care of his estate. He so buried himself in his books that he spent the nights reading from twilight till daybreak and the days from dawn till dark; and so from little sleep and much reading, his brain dried up and he lost his wits.

If you are developing a character, why not first create your own **SKETCH** for them (*see example below*). Then write a quick summary. Then you will be ready to attempt a full **CHARACTER PROFILE** (*next page*).

Character Sketch: Linton Heathcliff

Character name: Linton Heathcliff

Other names / Alias: The Boy / The Child; Maister Linton / Master Linton; The Young Master; Master Heathcliff / Idle Boy

Gender: Male

Nationality: English

Age: 13 years old (1797) 17 years old (death, 1801)

Home: London, England (birthplace). Lives at Wuthering Heights, Yorkshire, England

Relationships: Heathcliff (father); Isabella Linton (mother); Mr. Earnshaw (paternal grandfather; Hareton Earnshaw (cousin); Cathy Linton (cousin/wife)

Type: Deuteragonist Victim

Appearance: Pale, slim, frail, curly blonde hair, blue eyes

Personality: Weak, whiny, sickly, demanding, bratty, irritable, sensitive, charming, cruel, obedient, hateful, childish, fearful, gullible, rude, emotional, spoiled, exaggerative

Allies: Cathy Linton / Isabella Linton

Enemies: Heathcliff

Likes: Being with Cathy, writing letters to her and back, sitting in his chair, attention

Dislikes: Being treated cruelly by his father

Goal: To marry Cathy Linton for his father to claim ownership of Thrushcross Grange (succeeded)

Fate: Marries Cathy, but his health fails and dies shortly thereafter

CHARACTER PROFILES
why are they who they are?

You should now have everything you need to create a complex character and bring them to life in your narrative. If you want to go the extra mile and really get to know them before you start writing, then try completing a **CHARACTER PROFILE**. A good place to start is to make a **CHARACTER QUESTIONNAIRE**, like the one shown opposite. You can go deeper and organize this however you want, adding more categories as you see fit. Each time you create a significant new character simply ask them the same set of questions. There are also many pieces of software and worksheets available online which help writers to create profiles for their principal characters. Keep your initial questionnaire separate from your arcs (the ways your character will develop within the narrative).

Even if most of the information in a character profile does not appear in the story, it can guide a character's behavior and decision-making in the narrative. Thus, if your character as a child had an astronomer step-father, a talking pet parrot, and broke a leg while skiing, these experiences will color their interactions with older men, the cosmos, birds, intelligence, winter sports and snow. Portuguese writer Fernando Pessoa had a unique approach, creating signatures and astrology charts for his characters. There are of course limits to what is useful, though. As Salman Rushdie observes:

> In order to create one character, you would
> theoretically have to create the universe.

CHARACTER PROFILE QUESTIONNAIRE

Appearance

Name/age/gender/sexuality

Hair colour/eye colour/skin colour/build

Sociolect / dialect / loud or softly spoken

How do they dress? What do they sleep in?

Does your character wear glasses have tattoos/have any particular accessories?

Do they have any traits like tics, blinking, nail biting or constant humming?

Are they healthy? If so, why, if not, why not?

Do they have gentle face or an intimidating one?

What does this character do with their hands when talking?

How do they move?

Routines

What does your character do in the morning? Do they have a strict routine which they follow or is every day different?

What about going to bed?

Does your character cook? Do they eat at home often or do they have a favourite haunt?

What hobbies does your character have? Do they play violin like Sherlock Holmes, or Cello like Wednesday Aadams?

Do they run, or play squash, or like to dabble with Dungeons and Dragons?

Do they keep a diary or a calendar? Are they the kind of person to remember their niece's birthday?

Relationships

Does your character have siblings?

Are their parents still alive? Are they still together? What was/is your character's relationship with them like?

Do other people like your character or dislike them? Why?

How was school for this character?

What romantic relationships exist for your character?

Are they married, single, monogamous, celibate, promiscuous? What is their sexual orientation?

Who do they call when they need help or advice?

Do they have many friends? Are they many and varied, few, old, cliquey?

What kind of household did they grow up in? Was there conflict? What was the financial situation?

Personality

Are they an extrovert or an introvert? Gregarious or misanthropic?

Are they relaxed or anxious?

Are they outwardly positive?

Are they smart? How smart?

How kind, thoughtful, or aware are they?

How assertive, confident or decisive are they?

What makes your character happy?

What motivates them?

How organized are they?

How resilient is your character?

Does this character have a sense of humor or a strong temper?

What amuses or infuriates them?

Socio-economic

What is your character's level of education - scholar, graduate, self-made, not academic?

What is their class background - aristocracy, upper, upper middle, middle, lower middle, lower?

What is their economic situation - rich, independent, salaried, zero contract, dependent, unemployed?

What is your character's job or trade?

What is their group affiliation? Do they belong to or identify with a specific group or cultural genre?

Do they broadly feel accepted, rejected, or oppressed?

What is their political affiliation - Conservative, Socialist, Republican, Communist, Green, Anarchist?

Do they have a religious affiliation - Christian, Jewish, Muslim, Hindu, Buddhist, Hippie, Pagan, Atheist?

Psychological / Emotional

How creative are they? Highly original, conventional, or eccentric?

What do they think about themselves?

What do they think about the world?

Are they open-minded or closed-minded? Objective or subjective, generous or selfish, trusting or paranoid?

Where are their buttons or triggers?

What or whom do they love or value?

What do they deeply long for?

What do they need or lack?

What do they want or desire?

What is their goal?

What are their insecurities?

What do they fear most?

What are their weaknesses?

What are their flaws?

Do they have secrets?

What significant moments in their life made them who they are?

Are they prejudiced? If so what about?

Do they have fixed attitudes?

Did they change in the past? If so why?

How could they change in the future?

Moral / Ethical

How reliable is their moral compass?

What do they believe is right & wrong?

Can they tell right from wrong and make decisions based upon that knowledge?

How strong is their personal conscience? Is it stronger than what law or society dictates?

Does the character hold beliefs in contradiction to those around them?

Do they give a false perception of themselves to others?

How do their moral beliefs affect their conduct?

Are they involved in some kind of moral or ethical dilemma?

Are this character's beliefs likely to evolve and change in the future?

Is there a moral to their life so far?

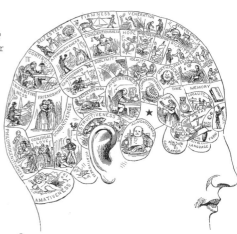